CRIME SCIENCE

ESPIONAGE

Matt Anniss

Gareth Stevens
Publishing

Please visit our website, www.garethstevens.com. For a free color catalog of all our high-quality books, call toll free 1-800-542-2595 or fax 1-877-542-2596.

Library of Congress Cataloging-in-Publication Data

Anniss, Matt.
Espionage / by Matt Anniss.
 p. cm. — (Crime science)
Includes index.
ISBN 978-1-4339-9489-0 (pbk.)
ISBN 978-1-4339-9490-6 (6-pack)
ISBN 978-1-4339-9488-3 (library binding)
1. Spies — Juvenile literature. 2. Intelligence service — United States — Juvenile literature. 3. Espionage — Juvenile literature. I. Anniss, Matt. II. Title.
JK468.I6 A56 2014
327.1273—dc23

First Edition

Published in 2014 by
Gareth Stevens Publishing
111 East 14th Street, Suite 349
New York, NY 10003

© 2014 Gareth Stevens Publishing

Produced by Calcium, www.calciumcreative.co.uk
Designed by Keith Williams and Paul Myerscough
Edited by Sarah Eason and Jennifer Sanderson

Photo credits: Cover: Shutterstock: Darrin Henry t, Gunnar Pippel b. Inside: Shutterstock: 36, Marcin Balcerzak 12, Peter Barrett 11b, BMCL 26, Denisenko 28, Elnur 5t, Featureflash 23, Frontpage 9, Fstockfoto 14, Gyn9037 38, Jorg Hackemann 4, ID1974 30, Ritu Manoj Jethani 7b, Rick Laverty 18, Zern Liew 11t, Lolloj 34, Mechanik 13, Monkey Business Images 40, MSPhotographic 5b, Muratart 19, Ollyy 1, 32, 41, Robert Pernell 29b, Petroos 35, Phil MacD Photography 22, Pressmaster 8, Alexander Raths 6, Alexander Ryabintsev 37b, Sashkin 37t, S.K Photography 45, Smileus 39, Subbotina Anna 44, Tommaso79 31, Oleg Yarko 20, Serg Zastavkin 10; Wikimedia Commons: BarryNL 27, Cherie Cullen 42, Israel Defense Forces 17, JohnsonL623 29t, Ryan Lawler 43, Marshall80 16, Axel Mauruszat 15t, Octahedron80 7t, Rama 24t, 25, U.S. Federal Government 21.

Printed in the United States of America

CPSIA compliance information: Batch #CS13GS: For further information contact Gareth Stevens, New York, New York at 1-800-542-2595.

CONTENTS

ESPIONAGE

Espionage is spying. It is a secretive world. It is the process of gaining sensitive or confidential information about another country or business rival without their permission, and ideally without them ever knowing.

The Science of Spying

The essence of espionage is gathering information. To do this, many governments use undercover spies—or secret agents, as they are popularly known. However, people sitting in offices do the majority of the work. To do their job, they rely on intelligence-gathering technology based on the latest cutting-edge science. This could be powerful radar listening stations, Internet-monitoring technology, or video cameras attached to satellites positioned high above Earth. Much of this technology was originally developed for the army, navy, and air force.

High-tech listening stations around the world help governments to gather information.

The ongoing threat of foreign spies on US soil was confirmed in June 2010, when the FBI announced that it had arrested suspected Russian secret agents. The suspected spies had been living undercover in the suburbs of New Jersey, Boston, and Seattle for at least 10 years before they were finally arrested.

Many secret agents spend their time trolling the Internet for information.

One Step Ahead

Being on top of the latest scientific developments is of vital importance to the espionage community. Staying one step ahead of your rivals—in most cases, other countries—and using science to your advantage is key to espionage success.

Traditional espionage work, including stealing secret documents, still goes on today.

CHAPTER ONE
THE WORLD OF ESPIONAGE

Espionage blurs the boundaries between what is legal and illegal in pursuit of information that could help prevent crime, terrorism, and war. Espionage work is undertaken by a wide range of people, from undercover spies to agents in office buildings.

Secret Agents

The main job of a secret agent is to go out and gather information about the activities of foreign governments. The United States' secret service is called the National Clandestine Service (NCS), and is operated by the CIA. The British equivalent is known as MI6, or the Secret Intelligence Service (SIS).

Scientists help the secret services by inventing tiny, high-tech gadgets for spies to use out in the "field."

CRACKED

One of the most frequently used gadgets in espionage is a "concealment device." This is an everyday item that has been modified to hide something. In 1953, the FBI discovered a hollowed-out nickel coin that had been used by Russian spies to hide microfilm containing secret codes.

Coins such as this hollow nickel found in 1958 have been used by spies to hide top-secret information.

Shadowy Figures

We do not know all that much about what spies are up to because their work is top secret. However, we do know that some spies are positioned in overseas embassies while others are issued with convincing cover stories. For example, they might pose as regular business people or top-level scientists. Being a spy is a dangerous job. If a spy's cover is blown, he or she could be killed.

Tiny Gadgets

The world's most famous imaginary spy, James Bond, is rarely without high-tech gadgets. While most of the gadgets shown in Bond movies are the work of someone's imagination, it is true that secret agents are often provided with ingenious gadgets. Over the years, these have included pens that write with invisible ink, hollowed-out books that hide USB memory sticks, and tiny radio transmitters.

Government offices overseas, known as embassies, hide spies and secret agents.

EMBASSY OF
THE UNITED STATES OF AMERICA

BACK AT HEADQUARTERS

The secret service headquarters of the most powerful countries in the world house an army of staff. Their job is to carry out routine surveillance to uncover any threat to the country's security.

Everyday Jobs

Most secret agents have quite uneventful jobs. Some are employed to monitor e-mails sent by suspected spies, listen to secret messages picked up by government listening stations, or communicate with agents based around the world.

Other agents are responsible for gathering all known information about a particular subject, such as attempts by rogue countries to build dangerous nuclear weapons. Some agents are responsible for keeping their country's president up to date about top-secret information.

Most people working in espionage are based in government offices around the world. Very few are secret agents.

Workers at the Pentagon in Washington organize much of the United States' espionage worldwide.

Double Agents

To become a secret agent, you have to pass vigorous security checks. This is to make sure that you are not likely to pass on information to the secret services of other nations. Over the years, many spies have been exposed as "double agents." These are agents who are employed by one agency, such as the CIA or MI6, but are secretly working for another. Double agents pose a huge risk because they often have access to highly sensitive information about national security.

REAL-LIFE CASE

One of the most famous double agents of all time was Chinese-American Larry Wu-tai Chin. He worked for the CIA between 1952 and 1985, first as an interpreter and then as an agent at the agency's headquarters in Langley, Virginia. During that time, he sold many secret documents to the Chinese. He was eventually tried and found guilty of spying in 1986.

INDUSTRIAL ESPIONAGE

Although we like to think of espionage as something only governments do, it is an increasing problem in the world of business. This kind of spying is known as industrial espionage. Its agents are responsible for stealing sensitive business information.

Cutthroat Business

The world of business is highly competitive, and some companies will stop at nothing to get ahead of their rivals. Industrial espionage is illegal because it usually involves stealing lists of customers, plans for new products, or information regarding the science behind cutting-edge technology.

If a company can get hold of this kind of information about its rivals, it may be able to use the information to launch similar products or gain some other competitive advantage. For example, if a rival computer company stole detailed plans for a new Apple computer, Apple could potentially lose billions of dollars.

Removable USB sticks have been used by industrial spies to steal product plans from top computer and weapons companies.

NO REMOVABLE MEDIA

Electromagnetic shielding is a new technique used to cut down on industrial espionage. All electrical equipment emits what is known as electrical radiation—invisible waves of energy. Sometimes, this radiation can give away vital information. Electromagnetic shielding prevents electrical radiation, ensuring no sensitive information seeps out.

In a bid to cut down on industrial espionage, some companies ban employees from using removable hard drives, such as USB sticks.

Government Interference

Some governments also take part in industrial espionage in order to steal or copy technology that they have not yet developed themselves. For example, it is thought that the Chinese Chengdu J-20 stealth fighter jet is based on a US F-117 Nighthawk plane. After an F-117 crashed in Serbia in 1999, it was reported that Chinese officials bought the remaining parts, which were then carefully studied. Eventually, the Chinese were able to design a new jet fighter with alarming similarities to the F-117.

The US government believes that Chinese spies have built war planes based on top-secret US technology.

CHAPTER TWO

WATCHING AND LISTENING

Secretive missions to kill enemy secret agents are a rarity. Most espionage work involves gathering information using a process called surveillance.

Surveillance Basics

Surveillance describes all activities that involve watching, listening, or monitoring. The secret services use a wide variety of surveillance techniques. They include "human intelligence" (things seen or heard by agents or informants), undercover filming, intercepting electronic communications (such as e-mails), and secretly recording telephone conversations.

Secretly watching somebody's movements is the most basic form of surveillance.

Advanced Technology

Over the last 100 years, the espionage community's thirst for information has led to many great technological advances. What originally starts out as top-secret technology often eventually becomes available to the public in another form. For example, we would not have satellite navigation in cars or location services on smartphones without military surveillance technology.

Location services on smartphones and satellite navigation in cars are based on technology originally created for use in espionage.

Bugging

Police forces now use surveillance techniques originally developed by the espionage community. It is not uncommon for police to record phone calls from suspects, or to place covert recording devices (known as bugs) in suspects' homes. "Bugging" is still widely used by secret agents. In the 1970s, Russian secret agents posing as laborers managed to plant hundreds of listening devices inside the walls of the US Embassy in Moscow. The US government eventually found so many bugs that the building had to be demolished and built again from scratch!

CRACKED

Bugs contain both a microphone and a tiny radio transmitter. When the device is switched on, it is possible to listen to private conversations from hundreds or even thousands of miles away. To avoid detection, these devices are usually small enough to easily be hidden inside other objects.

RADAR

Most modern surveillance technology has been built around a system called radar. Radar sends and receives waves of energy called radio waves. Radar systems are used in many different ways, from helping planes to reach their destination to listening out for covert messages from spies.

War Weapon

Radar systems were first used to detect enemy aircraft during World War II. Since then, radar has been developed for use in many different fields. Radar systems are used by weather forecasters to detect storms. Radar is also used to communicate with satellites high above Earth and also by submarines to figure out their exact location. Over the years, the US government has spent billions of dollars building radar stations all over the world. These include Ascension Island in the Atlantic Ocean and Opana Hill in Hawaii.

Enormous radar dishes can be used to listen to secret communications, such as telephone calls, from many thousands of miles away.

This abandoned radar station in Berlin was used by the US government during the Cold War to monitor Soviet telephone calls and radio communications.

Dual Purpose

Radar stations have two main purposes. The first is as an early-warning system against possible attack from the air (for example, by long-range missiles). The second is to scour the world for rogue communications that may be of assistance to the espionage community. The receivers used in radar stations are incredibly powerful. Sometimes, they look like enormous satellite dishes or oversized golf balls. They are capable of picking up stray radio transmissions from thousands of miles away.

CRACKED

Radar systems send and receive radio waves to figure out the exact location of objects (for example, airplanes or storm clouds). When radio waves sent from a radar transmitter hit an object, a certain amount will be deflected toward the transmitter. By measuring how long it takes for the deflected waves to return, radar systems can then figure out exactly where the object is.

SPY SATELLITES

Radar is not the only way governments keep tabs on the activities of other nations. Many countries, including the United States, China, and Russia, also own and operate a network of highly secretive spy satellites that are positioned high above Earth.

Watching Over Us

Spy satellites are effectively powerful telescopes. Instead of pointing toward outer space, they are pointed toward Earth. They are used to film or take photographs of enemy military bases, power stations, and communications buildings.

Sputnik and Corona

The first spy satellite, Sputnik, was launched by the Soviet Union in 1957. During the 1960s, the US government developed its own version, called Corona. Corona was used to take photos of Soviet missile sites. Since then, spy satellites have become much more powerful. They can now provide live film footage as well as photographs.

Since 1962, the Russians have sent nearly 2,500 Cosmos spy satellites into space.

Spy satellites take detailed photographs of foreign military sites and suspected terrorist training camps.

Old Technology

The only information we have regarding spy satellites is about old technology. It is not known how many US, Russian, or Chinese spy satellites are currently orbiting Earth. We also do not know exactly what the satellites are used for, although experts say that they are used just as much for intercepting communications as filming or taking photographs. On rare occasions, images taken by spy satellites will be shown to the public. This usually happens after successful military missions, such as the war against Iraq in 1990.

REAL-LIFE CASE

In 1984, three pictures taken by the top secret KH-11 spy satellite were published in a magazine called *Jane's Fighting Ships*. They had been sent to the magazine by Samuel Loring Morison, a US intelligence officer. He was sent to prison for two years after being convicted on two counts of espionage.

17

MESSAGES, MISSIONS, AND MICROWAVES

Spy satellite technology is usually "classified"—only those within the highest levels of government know about it. However, we do know that some satellites are used to listen in on enemy communications.

Listening In

Over the years, the US government has launched a number of spy satellites that were specifically designed to intercept Russian and Chinese communications. These listening satellites feature massive dishes, which reflect communications signals back toward Earth. The Aquacade spy satellites of the 1970s had reflective dishes around 65 feet (20 m) wide. USA-223, the spy satellite launched in 2010, reportedly has a radar dish more than 328 feet (100 m) wide. Insiders have described USA-223 as "the largest satellite ever built."

Huge rockets such as this one are needed to launch spy satellites into orbit.

Figuring It Out

Intercepting messages is one thing, but understanding them is another. Most top-secret messages are encrypted. This means that they are scrambled in some way or sent in a secret code. Even if these messages cannot be understood, there is still value in monitoring them.

Who and Why

Knowing who is sending and receiving messages, and how often, is almost as valuable as knowing what the message says. For example, it would be useful to know if two enemy states communicated regularly because it would suggest some kind of working relationship, or sharing of ideas.

Calls from cell phones are relayed around the world using a network of microwave radio masts.

A lot of secret communications are sent around the world using very short radio waves called microwaves. Although they are sent between top-secret sites using radar technology, some of the microwaves drift up into space. Some spy satellites have been designed to help intercept these messages by deflecting the signals back toward radar listening stations on Earth.

19

DRONES

In addition to spy satellites and radar listening stations, some governments also use Unmanned Aerial Vehicles (UAVs), better known as drones. These unmanned planes can fly close to the action for a bird's-eye view of proceedings.

Attack of the Drones

Drones are radio-controlled planes. A pilot sits in a room at a military base and controls the plane from there. Drones have a number of benefits over regular planes, including the ability to fly much closer to the ground.

Types of Drone

There are two main types of drone, those that carry weapons and are used by the military for remote attacks, and those that are unarmed. It is these unarmed drones that are used by the CIA and US military for espionage purposes.

The US government uses unmanned drone planes to spy on suspected terrorists around the world.

In May 2011, President Obama and his advisors watched live film footage sent by drones of the capture and killing of Osama bin Laden.

Live Footage

Unarmed drones are used almost exclusively for surveillance. They carry a number of different cameras for filming, including night vision. Night vision ensures good-quality pictures in the dark, something regular cameras cannot do. Pictures from drones are beamed live to government agents so that they can be analyzed. Drones have been used extensively by the United States in Afghanistan and Iraq to locate and kill terrorists.

REAL-LIFE CASE

Unarmed drones were used in the successful mission to find and kill Al-Qaeda leader Osama bin Laden. Drones were used to film bin Laden's compound in the months leading up to the raid in May 2011. On the night of the raid, they were also used to film the mission so that President Obama and his advisors could watch it unfold.

KEEPING TRACK OF THE WORLD

Although espionage is a secretive business, it is not uncommon for countries to share intelligence. In rare cases, two or more countries also join forces to gather intelligence.

Five Eyes

The biggest surveillance network that the public knows about is ECHELON. This is a joint partnership between the governments of the United States, the United Kingdom, Canada, New Zealand, and Australia.

A Vital Tool

ECHELON was established in the 1960s, at the very height of the Cold War. ECHELON is thought to be able to intercept communications sent all over the world via satellite, telephone, microwaves, and the Internet.

Many radar listening sites used as part of the ECHELON network feature buildings that look like giant golf balls.

Room 641A

We know that at least one Internet interception facility is being run by ECHELON. It is called Room 641A and is based in San Francisco. It is based at a site run by AT&T, through which a large proportion of the world's Internet traffic—such as e-mails, requests to access websites, and posts on social networking sites—flows.

NarusInsight

According to technicians that used to work at AT&T, the CIA installed a super-computer called NarusInsight. This computer is able to capture and analyze huge amounts of information in a matter of nanoseconds. It is likely that Room 641A is just one of a number of similar sites run by ECHELON around the world.

President Obama and British Prime Minister David Cameron meet to discuss security issues highlighted by the ECHELON network of listening stations.

CRACKED

The ECHELON system is simple to understand. A large number of radar listening stations and other surveillance facilities around the world are joined together using secure, top-secret communication links. The information captured by each facility—be it microwave communications, e-mails, or phone calls—is shared between each of the five ECHELON nations for espionage purposes.

CHAPTER THREE

CRACKING THE CODES

Governments know that spies or surveillance experts may intercept their top-secret messages, so many have developed ingenious secret codes or ways of hiding messages within other communications. This is known as cryptography.

Cryptography for Beginners

Although cryptography is thousands of years old, the basic principles are still the same. The idea is to create a system for writing messages that can be understood only by a very small number of people, specifically those who have a set of instructions. These instructions are known as a key. The key sets out the details of the code used, be it numbers instead of letters, random letters, or a combination of both.

These two devices are cryptographic tables once used by the Swiss army.

During World War II, the Germans used a special typewriter called the Enigma Machine to send secret, coded messages to generals in the field.

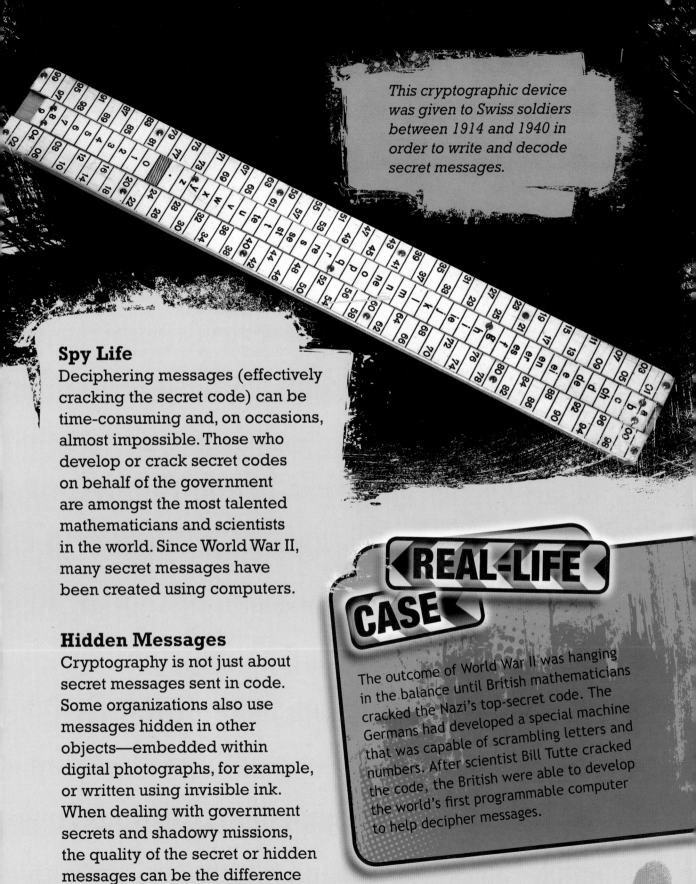

This cryptographic device was given to Swiss soldiers between 1914 and 1940 in order to write and decode secret messages.

Spy Life

Deciphering messages (effectively cracking the secret code) can be time-consuming and, on occasions, almost impossible. Those who develop or crack secret codes on behalf of the government are amongst the most talented mathematicians and scientists in the world. Since World War II, many secret messages have been created using computers.

Hidden Messages

Cryptography is not just about secret messages sent in code. Some organizations also use messages hidden in other objects—embedded within digital photographs, for example, or written using invisible ink. When dealing with government secrets and shadowy missions, the quality of the secret or hidden messages can be the difference between success and failure.

REAL-LIFE CASE

The outcome of World War II was hanging in the balance until British mathematicians cracked the Nazi's top-secret code. The Germans had developed a special machine that was capable of scrambling letters and numbers. After scientist Bill Tutte cracked the code, the British were able to develop the world's first programmable computer to help decipher messages.

25

THE SHORTWAVE SET

Communicating without arousing suspicion can be difficult, even for the best secret agents. One traditional method that is still in use is broadcasting seemingly random sets of numbers by shortwave radio. This is called a one-way voice link.

One-Way Link

At set times of the day, an unidentified voice will read out a set of numbers, in sequence, on a certain shortwave radio frequency. This system is known as a numbers station. In theory, anyone with a shortwave radio receiver can tune in, although nobody other than the spy being communicated with will be able to understand the message. The messages are written and deciphered using a one-time pad, which is said to be an unbreakable code system.

Mysterious numbers radio stations have been used by governments to send messages to secret agents since the 1940s.

Liberen a los Cinco
Free the Cuban five

¡Volverán!
They will retur[n]

Prisioneros en carceles norteamericanas
por luchar contra el terrorismo.
Anti-terroristm prisoners in North
American prisons

The Cuban Five are currently the only alleged spies ever arrested and tried for communicating via numbers stations.

REAL-LIFE CASE

In 1998, five Cuban spies were arrested in Florida and charged with espionage. At their trial, the FBI revealed that the five men had been given instructions using a numbers station nicknamed "Atención," operating out of Havana, Cuba. The FBI also found software used to decode the messages on one of the spies' laptop computers.

One-Time Pad

The one-time pad relies on spies being issued with a series of numbered key sheets containing random sets of five letters. Copies of the key sheets are also held by agents writing numbers broadcasts. Spies are told in advance, usually at the start of the broadcast, which numbered key sheet to use to decipher the message. The numbers read out in each broadcast seem random to untrained ears, but they actually represent different letters of the alphabet. Using basic math and the key sheet, the spy can easily figure out the message being broadcast.

HIDDEN MESSAGES

There are many ways to send secret messages. One of the most popular in espionage circles is steganography: the science of hiding messages in letters or pictures.

Invisible Ink

Traditionally, the most common form of steganography is the use of invisible ink. Most invisible inks are developed using chemicals. To reveal the hidden message, the spy may have to gently heat the paper, rub another chemical over the paper, or hold it under a special type of light. To conceal messages written in invisible ink, most spies will hide them within a regular letter. The "invisible" part may be written in the spaces between each line of the letter.

Spies often use invisible ink to hide messages inside seemingly ordinary letters.

This Microsoft logo, hidden inside a digital image in an instruction manual, is a good example of how photographs can be used to send messages.

Messages in Pictures

Today, computers are used to create hidden messages. One ingenious method is hiding messages inside digital pictures. These images are made up of hundreds of thousands of individual dots or square blocks, called pixels. By changing certain pixels, it is possible to send a message to someone. For example, each letter of the alphabet could be given a particular color. By changing every hundredth pixel to the color that corresponds to the letter of the alphabet, spies can conceal quite complicated messages in photos.

Using letters to send secret messages to spies is one of the oldest methods in the espionage toolbox.

CRACKED

It is now possible to buy specialist invisible ink for use in computer printers. This type of invisible ink, which can be seen under ultraviolet light, is widely used by the United States Postal Service to print invisible barcodes onto letters. By using machines that can read these invisible bar codes, they can sort the mail much more quickly.

THE COMPUTER AGE

The computer age has increased the importance of cryptography, not just in espionage, but also within our day-to-day lives. The passwords we use to protect our home computers are a low-level example of cryptography in action.

Password Protection

With a little knowledge, most computer passwords are easy to crack. However, the same cannot be said about the data-encryption techniques used by governments and secret agents to make sure their electronic communications are protected from prying eyes. Governments employ specialists in computer security to create forms of data encryption that are almost impossible to decipher. They also employ cryptanalysts, whose job it is to find weaknesses in other computer security systems.

Usernames and passwords, used to log in to Internet services such as e-mail, are a very basic example of encryption.

It is the job of cryptanalysts to stop vital, top-secret information from falling into the hands of terrorists and foreign spies.

Side-Channel Attacks

Cryptanalysts are usually computer scientists with a deep knowledge of math. As well as trying to find weaknesses in the computer systems used by other nations, they also test out the strength of their own government's systems. Some cryptanalysts take part in side-channel attacks, which are attempts to figure out the weaknesses in a security system by measuring the time it takes for a computer to perform a task, the amount of power used to perform a task, or the electrical radiation a computer emits.

CRACKED

A computer system that uses encrypted information to protect against hacking (see page 32) or send secret messages is known as a cryptosystem. An example would be a secure e-mail system, where messages can be sent and received only by two or more computers using the same encryption software. This software will encrypt, or scramble, the message when it is sent. Should the message fall into the wrong hands, it will not be understood.

CHAPTER FOUR

THE INFORMATION WAR

In the twenty-first century, many people believe that the greatest threat to our security does not come from traditional methods of espionage. Instead, it comes from those using advanced techniques to spy on us using computers. This is the world of cyberespionage.

Stalking the Internet

Cyberespionage is a growing problem. Most cyberespionage agents, or cyberspies, are experts in hacking. Hacking is the method of obtaining access to top-secret networks or breaking through security systems using specially created software. This malicious software, sometimes also called "malware," can be used to destroy computers, weaken security systems, and gain access to top-secret documents.

Most cyberspies evade detection by using their intimate knowledge of computer systems.

The US government believes that most cyberattacks against the United States originate in Southeast Asia.

Spying Today

In recent years, the number of incidents of attempted cyberespionage has increased dramatically. The US government believes that certain nations are behind some of the attacks, secretly employing top hackers to steal state secrets such as nuclear missile codes and military plans.

Mischief Makers

Governments also have to deal with cybercriminals, groups of hackers who just want to make mischief, and curious individuals. In 2002, a Scottish hacker named Gary McKinnon managed to gain access to top-secret NASA and CIA documents. He later claimed the hack was carried out to highlight weaknesses in US security.

CRACKED

One of the most dangerous pieces of software used by cyberspies is a Trojan horse. This is a piece of software that is hidden inside a seemingly normal e-mail attachment, such as a picture or MP3 file. When the recipient opens the attachment, the Trojan horse is installed. This allows the cyberspy to access the computer and steal important documents without the user's knowledge.

33

CYBERWARFARE

There is growing evidence that certain countries are deliberately setting out to hack into computers that belong to other nations not just to spy on them, but to also cause damage to the country's systems. This has become known as cyberwarfare.

Red Alert

The US government is so worried about the potential of cyberwarfare that it now classes the Internet as the "fifth theater of conflict" (the others are land, sea, air, and space). Seemingly, it has every right to be worried. In October 2012, the White House announced that hackers, reportedly working for the Chinese government, had gained access to top-secret information, potentially including nuclear missile command codes. Amazingly, this was achieved using a Trojan horse (see page 33).

Trojan horse malware, sent out by cyberspies and hackers, is a constant threat to the security of governments worldwide.

The US government believes the cyberspies and hackers may try to take control of the country's electricity supply by hacking into computers at power stations.

Targeting the Government

Cyberwarfare is the next step up from cyberespionage. Usually, cyberwarfare attacks are much larger and more persistent. They may come from many different sources at once, rather than a single computer or small network. Although they may have similar aims—for example, to steal government secrets—the aim of cyberwarfare is usually to weaken government "cyberdefenses."

Power Down

The US government is now worried that enemy states will use cyberwarfare to try to disrupt electrical power supplies. The government fears that the computers used to manage power stations will be targeted.

CRACKED

Cyberspies and hackers regularly use a technique called keylogging to record details of what people are typing into their computers. Once a hacker has gained access to a computer using a Trojan horse, he or she can install malware that records every key the user presses. The hacker can then read secret e-mails or documents as they are being written.

35

THE INVISIBLE THREAT

Cyberspies go to great lengths to hide their identity. As a result, finding out who is behind large-scale cyberwarfare attacks can be difficult. However, a lot of the evidence points to two countries that have difficult relations with the West—Iran and China.

Chinese Whispers

China may be a world superpower, but it still lags behind some Western countries in industries such as science, technology, and the manufacturing of weapons. Because of this, Chinese hackers regularly target the computer systems of US companies. Their aim is to steal information that could help them to develop their own rival software, gadgets, or weapons.

Operation Aurora

Beginning in October 2009, some of the United States' top banks and technology companies were targeted in cyberattacks. Called "Operation Aurora," the attacks included the theft of hundreds of thousands of passwords from Google e-mail accounts.

In 2009, leading Internet company Google was targeted by Chinese hackers in a huge cyberattack.

B44   Lobby

If you do not reinforce the security of your home Internet router box, it can be easy for cyberspies and hackers to steal your passwords.

Iran

In the past, the US government has launched cyberattacks against Iran. In 2010, hackers working for the CIA attacked the computer systems at several Iranian nuclear power stations. The US government hoped that this would slow attempts by Iran to build nuclear weapons. In 2012, the computer systems of a number of Western oil companies were attacked in what the US government claims was an act by the Iranian government.

Some famous cyberattacks on US companies and government computers have been traced to offices used by China's secret services.

REAL-LIFE CASE

Although the Chinese are thought to be behind many cyberespionage incidents, they also still use traditional methods of spying. In 2007, engineer Chi Mak was sent to prison for sending top-secret plans for US Navy ships to the Chinese government. He gained access to the plans while working for a Californian weapons company.

PICKING UP THE SIGNALS

Cyberspies hacking into government computer systems is not the only area of concern. It is also possible for secret agents to gain access to vital information from computers, using advanced scientific techniques.

Phreak Out

All electrical equipment gives off invisible waves of energy, called radiation. According to a scientist named Wim van Eck, it is possible to read any data displayed on a computer screen, or typed into a computer keyboard, if you have the technology to capture and analyze that computer's electrical radiation. He calls this technique of secretly "eavesdropping" on electrical radiation "Van Eck Phreaking." This is just one of the techniques that make it possible, although still difficult, to gain vital information and state secrets by recording and analyzing radiation.

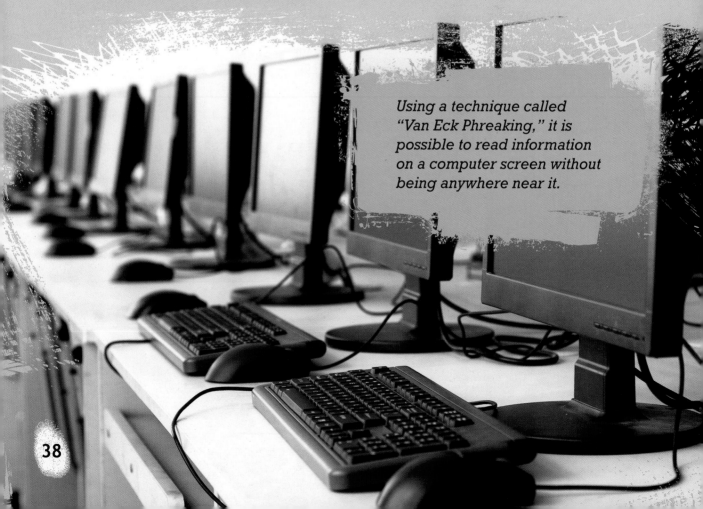

Using a technique called "Van Eck Phreaking," it is possible to read information on a computer screen without being anywhere near it.

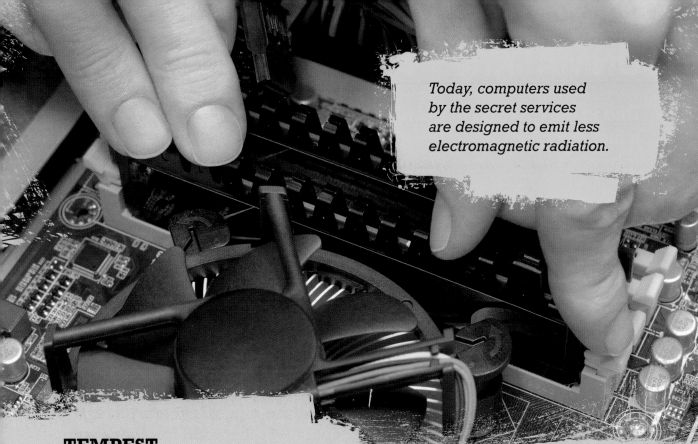

Today, computers used by the secret services are designed to emit less electromagnetic radiation.

TEMPEST

The US government has joined forces with other countries, such as the United Kingdom, to launch a program called TEMPEST. This top-secret program aims to develop ways of limiting the electrical radiation that is emitted by government computers. Scientists believe this will reduce any chance of enemy agents using Van Eck Phreaking techniques. The US Army has set up a TEMPEST testing laboratory at Fort Huachuca in Arizona.

Electromagnetic Shielding

One technique regularly used to protect computers is electromagnetic shielding. This effectively cuts down the level of radiation seeping out of computer equipment.

All computers used by the US government must be TEMPEST approved and built to certain specifications. These specifications include electromagnetic shielding around all components inside the computer that handle secret information. This is known as "Red/Black separation."

39

UNMASKING THE CYBERSPIES

Due to the growing threat of cyberespionage, a number of universities and companies have joined governments investing in cyberwarfare research. Their aim is to unmask the cyberspies who stalk the Internet.

Monitoring the Web

By far the most successful cyberespionage research project to date is InfoWar Monitor. Set up in 2002 and finally closed down in 2012, the project was funded by Canadian universities and technology companies. During that time, they were able to name governments found spying on their citizens, trace cyberespionage organizations, and point out major flaws in computer security systems all over the world. They won an enormous amount of praise for their efforts, which led to the unmasking of one of the biggest cyberespionage operations the world has ever seen.

A Canadian organization called InfoWar Monitor trained university students to successfully track down cyberspies.

Many hackers carry out their cyberattacks on behalf of foreign governments.

Ghost Town

After a year of research, InfoWar Monitor scientists were able to trace the origins of a large-scale cyberspying operation. The spy organization, codenamed GhostNet, attacked computers in government buildings around the world using a Trojan horse called Ghost Rat. This enabled GhostNet hackers to take control of computers and steal secret information. In total, GhostNet cyberspies attacked government computers in 103 different countries, including India, Canada, Germany, and the United States. InfoWar Monitor traced the source of the attacks to Hainan Island, China, home of a Chinese secret-service facility.

CRACKED

When researching GhostNet, InfoWar Monitor used a number of highly advanced techniques, including forensic computer analysis and laboratory testing, to trace the origins of the spy ring. During the investigation, it found that more than 1,295 computers had been affected by the Ghost Rat Trojan horse, giving cyberspies unprecedented access to state secrets.

PROTECTING THE UNITED STATES

Given the increase in cyberespionage attacks in recent years, it is no surprise that the United States government is taking the information war very seriously. In 2009, it set up a new department of the armed forces: CYBERCOM.

World First

Short for Cyber Command, CYBERCOM is based at Fort Meade, Maryland. It features representatives from the computer technology departments of all the major armed forces. Its role is to defend US government computer networks against cyberattacks and cyberespionage. On top of this, it is also charged with carrying out any aggressive cyberattacks against other nations ordered by the president. CYBERCOM was the world's first cyberwarfare organization. It also built the world's very first Cyberwarfare Intelligence Center, a kind of cyberespionage headquarters, at Lackland Air Force Base in Texas.

Commander of CYBERCOM Gen. Keith Alexander addresses the audience during the activation ceremony of CYBERCOM.

CYBERCOM believes that cyberspies and hackers may target computers at the New York Stock Exchange.

Counterintelligence

Although CYBERCOM has a role in fighting cyberespionage, it is largely concerned with cyberwarfare. In fact, the CIA handles a lot of the US government's cyberespionage work. The organization's Counterintelligence Center Analysis Group was first set up to identify and analyze the efforts of foreign intelligence agencies (secret-service organizations run by other countries). As well as monitoring traditional espionage activities, it now handles cyberespionage. The CIA still puts more resources into dealing with terrorism, but cyberespionage may now be a greater risk.

BACK IN THE LAB

There is little information about what CYBERCOM does. It is thought that its agents divide their time between rigorously testing military computer systems, developing new methods to combat the cyberwarfare threat, and launching secret cyberattacks against enemy nations.

43

SCIENTIFIC "ARMS RACE"

The methods used by spies and secret agents may have changed over the last 50 years, but espionage remains a huge problem for governments and businesses around the world. The threat from cyberespionage will continue to rapidly grow.

As long as governments disagree, there will always be secret agents and cyberspies.

The Science of Spying

Both science and technology play a huge role in espionage. Over the years, competing nations have been involved in a scientific arms race to develop new forms of surveillance technology. All major nations, wherever they are based in the world, have their own secret intelligence operations. Some are bigger than others, but all have the same aim: to steal secrets using a variety of advanced methods.

In 2011, a dispute erupted between the French president (above) and the US government over alleged "bugging" by US spies.

Next Generation

While secret agents may still use traditional espionage methods, in the future, cyberespionage will become increasingly important. That means that many of the world's best computer scientists will be needed to develop new methods of protection against cyberattacks. It is likely that countries will also actively seek out the world's most devious hackers to help them launch secret cyberattacks against their rivals. Where once countries relied on spies living undercover around the world, in the future they will rely more on computer experts to find and steal the information they need.

REAL-LIFE CASE

In November 2012, sources close to the French secret services accused US secret agents of a cyberattack that helped them gain access to confidential information about the French president. They claim that undercover CIA agents befriended the president's staff on Facebook, in order to "infect" French government computers with malicious Trojan horse software.

45

GLOSSARY

CIA Central Intelligence Agency, the United States' security service. It carries out most of the government's espionage work.

clandestine secretive

communications messages between people. These can take many forms, such as phone calls, e-mails, radio transmissions, and letters.

conceal to hide

cryptanalyst someone who specializes in cryptography

cryptography the science of writing and reading secret messages

data information

decipher to understand the meaning of secret messages

decode to figure out a message sent in secret code

devious crooked, underhanded

embassies government offices abroad

encrypt to turn something into secret code. Passwords are a form of encryption.

hacker a computer specialist who tries to gain access to computer networks for illegal purposes

intercepting getting hold of, seeing, or hearing something before it reaches its intended target

malicious intended to do harm

malware computer software designed to cause damage to another computer or series of computers

microfilm a much smaller version of photographic film, used to store tiny copies of information

nanoseconds billionths of a second

nuclear power a way to create electricity by using the energy stored in atoms

nuclear weapons dangerous, highly powerful weapons capable of destroying an entire town or city

orbiting moving around a planet

radar a system used to send and receive signals or messages using radio waves, usually with the purpose of locating a particular object

satellite a man-made device sent into space for a specific purpose

shortwave radio a type of radio broadcast that sends out very short radio waves. Because of this, shortwave radio broadcasts can be picked up thousands of miles away.

software something on a computer designed to do a specific task

Soviet Union a formerly communist country in eastern Europe and northern Asia. It included Russia and 14 other soviet socialist republics.

super-computer a computer that is thousands of times more powerful than an average home PC

transmission the broadcast of something, such as radio or television programs

unprecedented never happened before

USB memory stick a portable device used for storing computer data, files, and other electronic information

FOR MORE INFORMATION

BOOKS

Fridell, Ron. *Spy Technology.* New York, NY: Lerner Publications, 2007.

Gifford, Clive. *Espionage and Disinformation.* Chicago, Il: Heinemann, 2006.

Gifford, Clive. *Spies.* London, UK: ABC Books, 2007.

WEBSITES

Find out more about the work of the CIA and what you need to do to work there at:
www.cia.gov/kids-page/

Listen to genuine recordings of secret broadcasts by shortwave radio "numbers stations" run by the secret services at:
archive.org/details/ird059

Find out more about the work of MI5, part of the British secret service at:
www.mi5.gov.uk/home/the-threats/espionage.html

Find out more about the secret services and top-secret spying techniques. You can try spying methods out for yourself at:
www.topspysecrets.com

INDEX